MOONSHINE

DREAMWORKS ARTISTS...AFTER DARK!

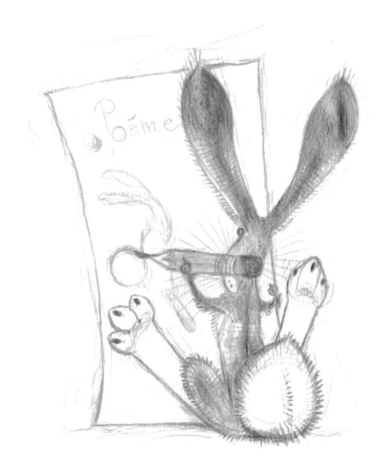

MOONSHINE
DreamWorks Artists...After Dark!

Published by
Design Studio Press
8577 Higuera Street
Culver City, CA 90232

Web site: www.designstudiopress.com
E-mail: info@designstudiopress.com
10 9 8 7 6 5 4 3 2 1

Printed in Korea
First edition, September 2010

Paperback ISBN 978-1-933-492-94-0
Library of Congress Control Number 2010931955

TABLE of CONTENTS

FOREWORD

Working in animation, I find myself in the company of artists every day. I have become accustomed to traveling hallways bedecked with an ever-changing array of drawings and paintings—character designs, backgrounds, and development art from our films. A gallery of artists working toward a common goal, blending their individual talents together on a huge scale.

But concentrations of talent this large are rare. No one starts their artistic life in such a huge community. Even if the people who work here were born in crowded urban centers, they were likely isolated as artists. Because artists occur unpredictably, blossoming randomly within a population as surprises of nature.

I once asked a group I worked with to bring in works they created as children so that I could display these early artistic explorations in a gallery show. To my surprise, at the age of only three or four, future painters were already working with brushes and color while animators and character designers had gravitated to pencils and paper. They had already discovered their art, and they were well on their way to define and expand it.

So every artist here developed their styles according to their own gifts, in isolation. In peace and quiet. Developing their art without distraction. Skills formed at a time when everyone drew and painted for the joy of it, while they were in clear contact with the deepest part of themselves, blissfully unaware that they might someday rely on these gifts to make a living. Unique styles that have only strengthened with time.

During the day, these artists carefully coordinate their skills in cooperative effort, weaving their individual colors together to create huge tapestries. But they still retain the purity of a voice they discovered long ago. Strong, clear voices singing together in a choir.

But even if you sing in a choir, you never stop singing in the shower. That's still the time when the best singing happens. Times when you don't need to blend with anyone else. When you stay in touch with whatever started you singing in the first place.

So that is what this book is about. Voices from a choir singing on their own.

—Chris Sanders
Director of *Lilo & Stitch* and *How to Train Your Dragon*

"A stolen ear of corn has a better taste than one that is bought!"

That's an old saying in the countryside where I grew up. And it's true, isn't it? The ear of corn you buy tastes of a bought ear of corn, there's no denying it. The stolen one, on the other hand, tastes of running, adrenalin, off-limits!!

The works of art in *Moonshine* taste of the stolen corn of my childhood...The paintings, drawings, and doodles of this book are personal works from the visual development artists at DreamWorks.

These works were born after dark, when shadows win over light, after long days on productions like *Shrek*, *Madagascar*, *Kung Fu Panda*, and *How to Train Your Dragon*.

That's when pencils bustle, under the yellowish light of a desk lamp...next to the mug of cold coffee used now to clean brushes!

These artistic ninjas unveil their works of art hidden from the public eye until now; forbidden in broad daylight, stashed so long under their folded elbows that even the moon was not allowed a peek!

Moonshine is this 120-page book you can steal from your friends to savor under a tree.

—Christophe Lautrette
Moonshine Co-editor and Production Designer
DreamWorks Animation

Christian Schellewald

(clockwise from top left)

Bangkok
Pen and digital

Sunset Blvd
Pen and digital

Ventura Blvd
Pen and oil on board

NEW SUNSET BLVD   6 PM.

THE THIRD PLACE

SCHELLEWALD 07

Christian Schellewald

Datsun
Ink and acrylic paint on wood

Evergreen
Ink and acrylic paint on wood

Nicolas Marlet

Untitled
Colored pencil

Untitled
Colored pencil
and gouache

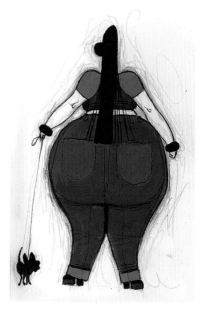
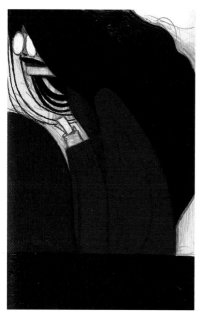

Nicolas Mar[

Untitled
Colored penci[
and gouache

Untitled
Colored penci[
and gouache

Devin Crane

An Angel in Versace
Acrylic and oil on wood

Shoe Heaven
Acrylic and oil on wood

Devin Crane

Don't Break My Heart
Acrylic and oil on wood

Waiting in Klimt
Acrylic

Alex Puvilland

Untitled
Ink and digital

Untitled
Ink and digital

Griselda Sastrawinata

Thio Sin Lian
Acrylic on panel

Guitar Lesson
Acrylic on panel

Goro Fujita

The Chase
Digital painting

The Show
Digital painting

Tang Kheng Heng

Drain Pipe
Acrylic on panel

Tang Kheng Heng

N35
Oil on panel

The Road
Acrylic on panel

The Encounter
Acrylic on panel

Nathan Fowkes

Flowers
Charcoal on paper

Angeles Crest
Watercolor on Arches paper

Iguana
Watercolor on Arches paper

Nathan Fowkes

Jerusalem
Watercolor on illustration board

Bridesmaid
Charcoal on paper

Ritche Sacilioc

Steady
Digital painting

Ritche Sacilioc

Steady
Digital painting

Emil Mitev

Friends 01
Gouache and graphite

Friends 02
Watercolor and graphite

Toro 02
Watercolor and graphite

Ronald Kurniawan

Extinction
Acrylic

Ronald Kurniawan

Car Sick
Acrylic

Baboon on an Island
Acrylic

Nicolas Weis

Le roi crabe
Walnut ink, watercolor, and gouache

Never Surrender
Walnut ink, watercolor, and gouache

Sylvain Deboissy

Untitled
Digital painting

Untitled
Digital painting

Bryan Gregg LaShelle

Untitled
Acrylic

Untitled
Digital painting

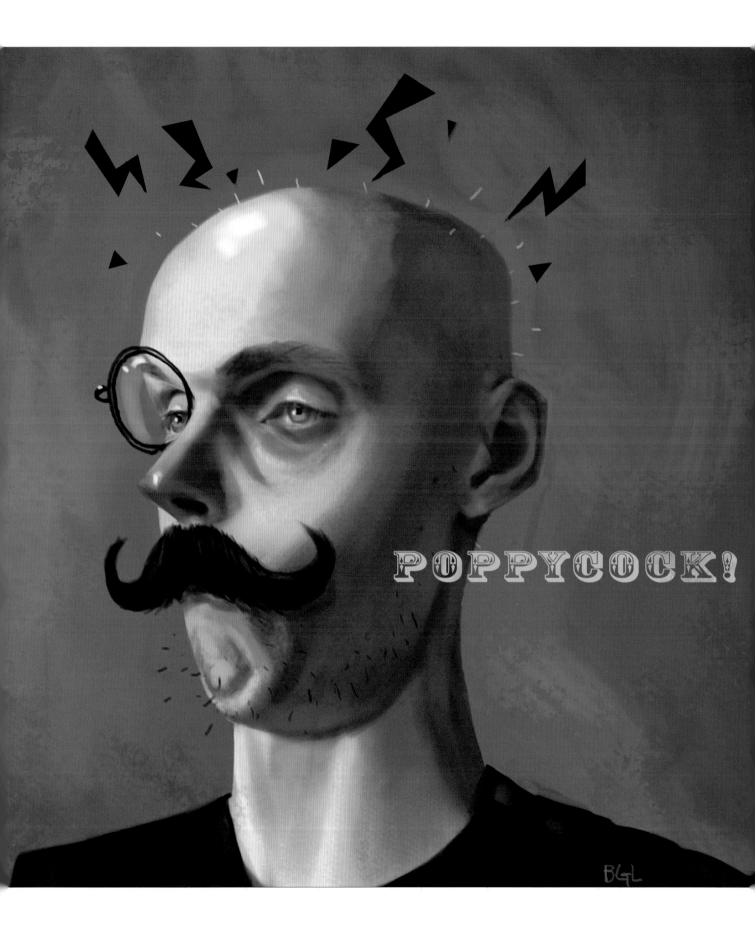

AahLo.

Shane Prigmore

Aahlo
Pencil and digital

SHANE
PRIGMORE

Paul Lasaine

Prague
Acrylic on Masonite

Venice
Digital painting

SAMUEL
MICHLAP © 2001

Samuel Michlap

Upper Level
Oil on board

opposite:

State and Washington
Oil on board

previous pages:

Samuel Michlap

Seattle Harbor
Gouache on board

Bruck Braid
Ink on paper

Christophe Lautrette

Ze Cow-Boy
Pencil and watercolor

Bazaar!
Mixed media

Les Mysteres
DE L'UNIVERS.

LES 3 IDIOTS

DES LARMES
de
CROCODILE

MÊME PAS MAL...

AAH, LA LUNE,
QUAND MÊME.

Christophe Lautrette

Good or Bad?
Digital painting

1910
Pencil and digital

Nate Wragg

A Long Week
Acrylic and collage

No Wind & No Friends
Acrylic and collage

Sasquatch Squalor
Acrylic and collage

Shannon Tindle

Zheng He's Return
Digital painting

The Maid
Digital painting

previous pages:
Pierre-Olivier Vincent

The Departure of the Calypso
Digital painting

Sunil Pant

The Meek Shall Inherit
Digital painting

Alex Hagelis

Distill
Digital painting

opposite:

Todd Gibbs

The Wingman
Digital painting

Felix Yoon

Scare Tree
Digital painting

Distant Peak
Digital painting

Ruben Perez

Early Dream 1
Digital painting

Early Dream 2
Digital painting

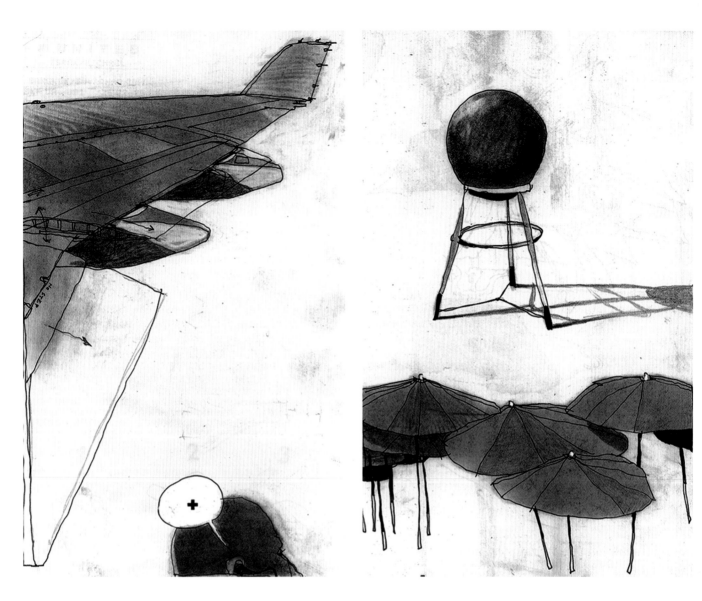

previous pages:

Michael Isaak

Untitled
Ink and charcoal

Michael Isaak

Untitled
Ink and charcoal

Untitled
Ink and charcoal

Marcos Mateu-Mestre

Alley Market
Digital painting

Marcos Mateu-Mestre

The Cast
Digital painting

Dominique Louis

Zyra
Digital painting

Chin Ko

Robots
Digital painting

City
Digital painting

Shannon Jeffries

Dream No. 11,683
Acrylic paint and digital paint

Untitled
Acrylic paint and digital paint

Kirsten Kawamura

Untitled
Digital painting

Untitled
Digital painting

Untitled
Digital painting

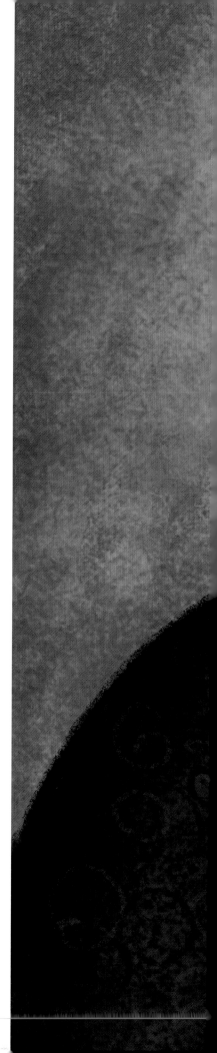

Simon Rodgers

Deep
Digital painting

Salvage
Digital painting

Lindsey Olivares

Meet You at the Living Room
Digital painting

Iuri Lioi

Back Alley
Digital painting

Tianyi Han

Black Forest
Pen and ink and digital

Paul Duncan

Bryce Study
Oil painting

Millard Creek
Oil painting

Jason Brubaker

Denny's
Pencil on paper, scanned painted textures

reMIND
Pencil on paper, scanned painted textures

Bill Kaufmann

Solitude
Pastel

Dragon Night
Pastel

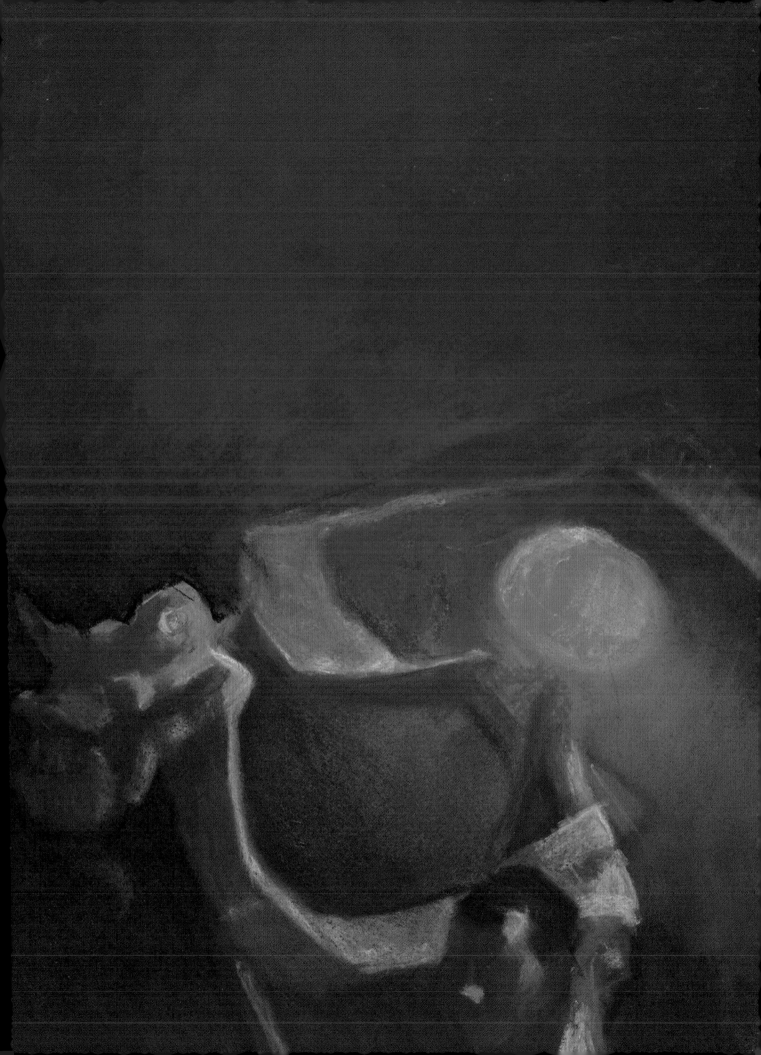

Max Boas

Untitled
Acrylic

Untitled
Acrylic

Untitled
Acrylic

Ruben Hickman

Los Angeles
Acrylic and charcoal on paper

Los Angeles
Acrylic and charcoal on paper

Ruben Hickman
Los Angeles
Acrylic and charcoal on paper

Jason William Scheier

Sleeping Giant
Digital painting

Untitled
Digital painting

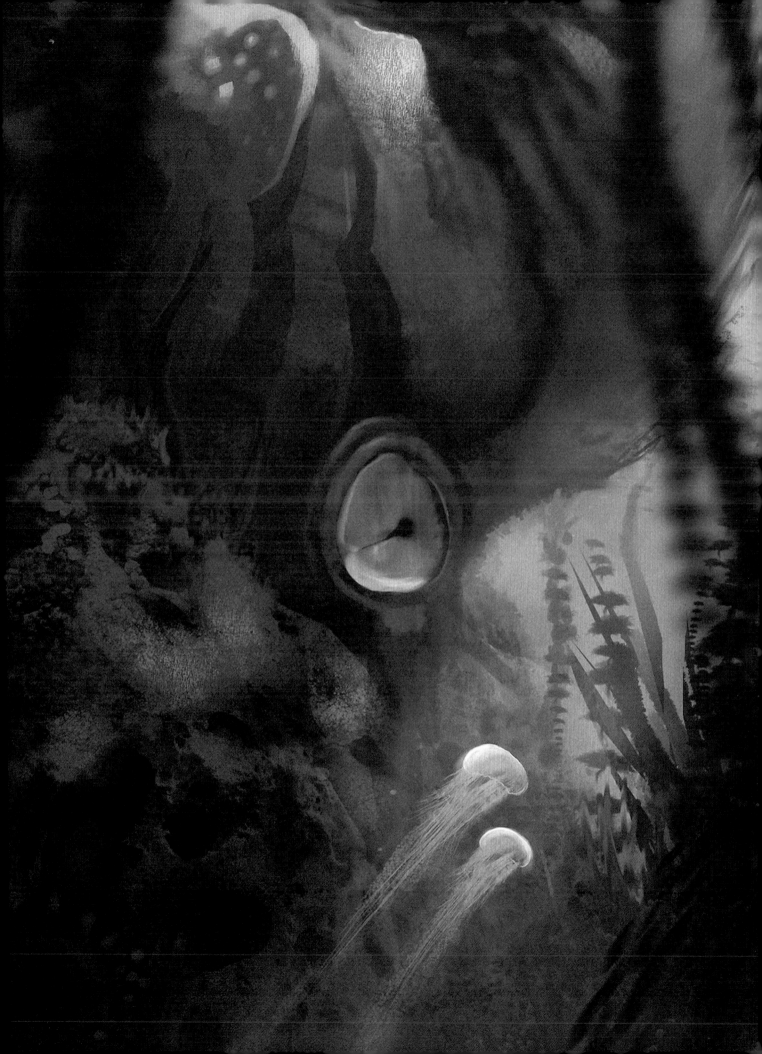

ZhaoPing Wei

The Secret Stream
Oil on canvas

Winter Scape
Oil on canvas

ZhaoPing Wei

Crystal Cove
Oil on canvas

Portrait of a Tibetan Woman
Oil on canvas

Leighton Hickman

Speakeasy
Digital painting

Drive-By
Digital painting

Jon Klassen

Up to the House
Collage and digital

Waterfall
Collage and digital

Patrick Mate

A cookie, Mirabelle?
Pencil drawing, digital painting

Poker Dog
Pencil drawing, digital painting

Job Inquiry
Pencil drawing, digital painting

Patrick Mate

Stork Airline
Pencil drawing and digital painting

Barry Pacific
Pencil drawing and digital painting

Chris Applehans

Untitled
Watercolor

Moonshine is a window through which you may tiptoe to see the work of our artists without being seen. It is down on one knee that I thank our participating DreamWorks artists for revealing a hint of their private lives.
Thank you for letting us peek into your workshops and your imagination. I'm sure through all the racket of ruffled paper, squashed leads, and cap-less paint tubes, there are still treasures to unveil! Keep the cleaning staff at bay so that all those little mice in the world can have the most of it.

I dedicate this book to my sons, Nolan and Devin, and my beautiful wife, Bernie. The book is inspired by my father's eye for detail, my mother's big heart, and my brother's creative mind.

"Un grand merci" to Benedicte Guenoden and Vy Trinh for their precious help.

See you soon,

—Christophe Lautrette
Moonshine Co-editor and Production Designer
DreamWorks Animation

A very special thanks to Joty Lam, my personal guardian angel and DreamWorks which in many ways while far away from my native country became my new home.

—Pierre-Olivier Vincent
Moonshine Co-editor and Art Director
DreamWorks Animation

I would like to thank Christophe and POV for championing this project and going above and beyond to realize it. A special thanks to John Tarnoff, who laid the groundwork for it. We would also like to thank the following DreamWorks folks for their gracious support of it: Ann Daly, Bill Damaschke, Dan Satterthwaite, Gail Currey, Todd Whitford, Katherine O'Connor, Brian Smith, Jonathan Lee, Daniel Kwan, Adrienne Steinbaum, Jackie Huang and Lauren Malizia. Finally, we would like to thank Jeffrey Katzenberg for creating an inspiring space where art may happen.

Angela Lepito
Production Manager
DreamWorks Animation

ARTIST INDEX and CONTACT INFO

selected other titles by design studio press:

The Skillful Huntsman
ISBN 0-9726-6764-4

Alien Race
ISBN 978-1-93349-223-0

Entropia
ISBN 978-1-93349-204-9

The Daily Zoo
ISBN 978-1-93349-232-2

LA<>SF
ISBN 1-933492-10-4

Luminair
ISBN 1-9334922-4-4

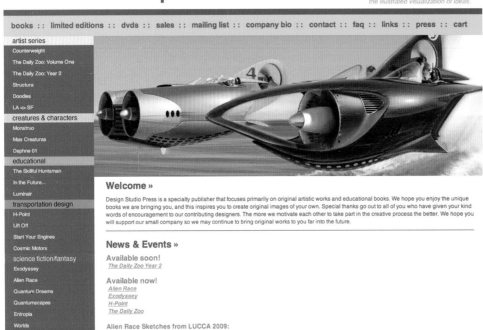
To order additional copies of this book and to view other books we offer, please visit:
www.designstudiopress.com

For volume purchases and resale inquiries, please e-mail:
info@designstudiopress.com

To be notified of special sales discounts throughout the year, please sign up to our mailing list at:
www.designstudiopress.com

Or you can write to:

Design Studio Press
8577 Higuera Street
Culver City, CA 90232

tel 310.836.3116
fax 310.836.1136

designstudio PRESS